SELF-IMPROVEMENT

101

WHAT EVERY LEADER NEEDS TO KNOW

JOHN C. MAXWELL

THOMAS NELSON
Since 1798

NASHVILLE   DALLAS   MEXICO CITY   RIO DE JANEIRO   BEIJING

Published in Nashville, Tennessee, by Thomas Nelson. Thomas Nelson is a registered trademark of Thomas Nelson, Inc.

Published in association with Yates & Yates, www.yates2.com.

Thomas Nelson, Inc., titles may be purchased in bulk for educational, business, fund-raising, or sales promotional use. For information, please e-mail SpecialMarkets@ ThomasNelson.com.

Portions of this book have been previously published in *Your Road Map for Success, Talent Is Never Enough, Developing the Leaders Around You, Failing Forward, The 360° Leader, Winning with People*, and *Leadership Gold* by John C. Maxwell.

Library of Congress Cataloging-in-Publication Data

Maxwell, John C., 1947–
    Self-improvement 101 : what every leader needs to know / John C. Maxwell.
        p. cm.
    Includes bibliographical references.
    ISBN 978-1-4002-8024-7
    1. Leadership. 2. Self-actualization (Psychology) I. Title.
    HD57.7.M39428 2009
    658.4'092—dc22

                                                                            2009028418

Printed in the United States of America

09 10 11 12 13 WC 6 5 4 3 2 1

Contents

PREFACE

I've been passionate about personal growth for most of my life. In fact, I've created and pursued a plan for growth every year for the last forty years! People say that wisdom comes with age. I don't believe that's true. Sometimes age comes alone. I wouldn't have achieved any of my dreams had I not been dedicated to continual improvement. If you want to grow and become the best person you can be, you've got to be intentional about it.

At the same time, life is busy and complex. Most people run out of day long before their to-do lists are done. And trying to get to the bottom line in just about any area of life can be a challenge. Did you know that more new information has been produced in the last thirty years than in the previous five thousand? A single weekday edition of the *New*

York Times contains more information than most people in seventeenth-century England were likely to encounter in their lifetimes.

That's why we've developed this series of 101 books. We've cherry-picked the essentials in subjects such as leadership, attitude, relationships, teamwork, and mentoring and put them into a format that you very likely can read in one sitting. Or you can easily toss a 101 book into a briefcase or purse and read here and there as time allows.

In many of my larger books, I go into my subject in great depth. I do that because I believe it is often the best way to add value to people. *Self-Improvement 101* is different. It is an introduction to a subject, not the "advanced course." But I believe it will help you on your way to significant growth in this area of your life.

PART I

LAYING A FOUNDING FOR SELF-IMPROVEMENT

WHAT WILL IT TAKE FOR ME TO IMPROVE?

*Growth must be intentional—
nobody improves by accident.*

The poet Robert Browning wrote, "Why stay we on the earth except to grow?" Just about anyone would agree that growing is a good thing, but relatively few people dedicate themselves to the process. Why? Because it requires change, and most people are reluctant to change. But the truth is that without change, growth is impossible. Author Gail Sheehy asserted:

If we don't change, we don't grow. If we don't grow, we are not really living. Growth demands a temporary surrender of security. It may mean a giving up of familiar but limiting patterns, safe but unrewarding work, values no longer believed in, relationships that have lost their meaning. As Dostoevsky put it, "taking a new step, uttering a new word, is what most people fear most." The real fear should be the opposite course.

I can't think of anything worse than living a stagnant life, devoid of change and improvement.

Growth Is a Choice

Most people fight against change, especially when it affects them personally. As novelist Leo Tolstoy said, "Everyone thinks of changing the world, but no one thinks of changing himself." The ironic thing is that change is inevitable. Everybody has to deal with it. On the other hand, growth is optional. You can choose to grow or fight it. But know this: people unwilling to grow will never reach their potential.

In one of his books, my friend Howard Hendricks asks the question, "How have you changed . . . lately? In the last week, let's say? Or the last month? The last year? Can you be *very specific*?" He knows how people tend to get into a rut when it comes to growth and change. Growth is a choice, a decision that can really make a difference in a person's life.

Most people don't realize that unsuccessful and successful people do not differ substantially in their abilities. They vary in their desires to reach their potential. And nothing is more effective when it comes to reaching potential than commitment to personal growth.

PRINCIPLES FOR SELF-IMPROVEMENT

Making the change from being an occasional learner to becoming someone dedicated to personal growth goes against the grain of the way most people live. If you asked one hundred people how many books they have read on their own since leaving school (college or high school), I bet only a handful would say they have read more than one or two books. If you asked how many listen to audio lessons and voluntarily attend conferences and seminars to grow personally, there would be even fewer. Most people celebrate when they receive their diplomas or degrees and say to themselves, "Thank goodness that's over. Just let me have a good job. I'm finished with studying." But such thinking doesn't take you any higher than average. If you want to be successful, you have to keep growing.

As someone who has dedicated his life to personal growth and development, I'd like to help you make the leap to becoming a dedicated self-developer. It's the way you need to go if you want to reach your potential. Besides that, it also has another benefit: it brings contentment. The happiest people I know are growing every day.

Take a look at the following eight principles. They'll help you develop into a person dedicated to personal growth:

1. Choose a Life of Growth

It's said that when Spanish composer-cellist Pablo Casals was in the final years of his life, a young reporter asked him, "Mr. Casals, you are ninety-five years old and the greatest cellist that ever lived. Why do you still practice six hours a day?"

What was Casals's answer? "Because I think I'm making progress." That's the kind of dedication to continual growth that you should have. The people who reach their potential, no matter what their profession or background, think in terms of improvement. If you think you can "hold your ground" and still make the success journey, you are mistaken. You need to have an attitude like that of General George Patton. It's said that he told his troops, "There is one thing I want you to remember. I don't want to get any messages saying we are holding our position. We are advancing constantly." Patton's motto was, "Always take the offensive. Never dig in."

The only way to improve the quality of your life is to improve yourself. If you want to grow your organization, you must grow a leader. If you want better children, you must become a better person. If you want others to treat you more kindly, you must develop better people skills. There is no sure way to make other people in your environment improve. The only thing you truly have the ability to improve is yourself. And the amazing thing is that when you do, everything else around you suddenly gets better. So the bottom line is that if you want to take the success journey, you must live a life of growth. And the only way you will grow is if you *choose* to grow.

2. Start Growing Today

Napoleon Hill said, "It's not what you are going to do, but it's what you are doing now that counts." Many unsuccessful people have what I call "someday sickness" because they could do some things to bring value to their lives right now. But they put them off and say they'll do them *someday*.

Their motto is "One of these days." But as the old English proverb says, "*One* of these days means *none* of these days." The best way to ensure success is to start growing today. No matter where you may be starting from, don't be discouraged; everyone who got where he is started where he was.

Why do you need to determine to start growing today? There are several reasons:

- *Growth is not automatic.* In my book *Breakthrough Parenting,* I mention that you can be young only once, but you can be immature indefinitely.[1] That's because growth is not automatic. Just because you grow older doesn't mean you keep growing. That's how it is with some creatures, such as crustaceans. As a crab or a lobster ages, it grows and has to shed its shell. But that's not the trend for people. The road to the next level is uphill, and it takes effort to keep growing. The sooner you start, the closer to reaching your potential you'll be.

- *Growth today will provide a better tomorrow.* Everything you do today builds on what you did yesterday. And altogether, those things determine what will happen tomorrow. That's especially true in regard to growth. Oliver Wendell Holmes offered this insight: "Man's mind, once stretched by new ideas, never regains its original dimensions." Growth today is an investment for tomorrow.

- *Growth is your responsibility.* When you were a small child, your parents were responsible for you—even for your growth and education. But as an adult, you bear that responsibility entirely. If you don't make growth your responsibility, it will never happen.

There is no time like right now to get started. Recognize the importance that personal growth plays in success, and commit yourself to developing your potential today.

3. FOCUS ON SELF-DEVELOPMENT, NOT SELF-FULFILLMENT

There has been a change in focus over the last thirty years in the area of personal growth. Beginning in the late sixties and early seventies, people began talking about "finding themselves," meaning that they were searching for a way to become self-fulfilled. It's like making happiness a goal because self-fulfillment is about feeling good.

But self-development is different. Sure, much of the

time it will make you feel good, but that's a by-product, not the goal. Self-development is a higher calling; it is the development of your potential so that you can attain the purpose for which you were created. There are times when that's fulfilling, but other times it's not. But no matter how it makes you feel, self-development always has one effect: It draws you toward your destiny. Rabbi Samuel M. Silver taught that "the greatest of all miracles is that we need not be tomorrow what we are today, but we can improve if we make use of the potential implanted in us by God."

4. NEVER STAY SATISFIED WITH CURRENT ACCOMPLISHMENTS

My friend Rick Warren says, "The greatest enemy of tomorrow's success is today's success." And he is right. Thinking that you have "arrived" when you accomplish a goal has the same effect as believing you know it all. It takes away your desire to learn. It's another characteristic of destination disease. But successful people don't sit back and rest on their laurels. They know that wins—like losses—are temporary, and they have to keep growing if they want to continue being successful. Charles Handy remarked, "It is one of the paradoxes of success that the things and ways which got you there are seldom those things that keep you there."

No matter how successful you are today, don't get complacent. Stay hungry. Sydney Harris insisted that "a winner knows how much he still has to learn, even when he is considered an expert by others; a loser wants to be considered an expert by others before he has learned enough to know how little he knows." Don't settle into a comfort zone, and don't let success go to your head. Enjoy your success briefly, and then move on to greater growth.

5. BE A CONTINUAL LEARNER

The best way to keep from becoming satisfied with your current achievements is to make yourself a continual learner. That kind of commitment may be rarer than you realize. For example, a study performed by the University of Michigan several years ago found that one-third of all physicians in the United States are so busy working that they're two years behind the breakthroughs in their own fields.[2]

If you want to be a continual learner and keep growing throughout your life, you'll have to carve out the time to do it. You'll have to do what you can wherever you are. As Henry Ford said, "It's been my observation that most successful people get ahead during the time other people waste."

That's one reason I carry books and magazines with me whenever I travel. During the downtimes, such as waiting for a connection in an airport, I can go through a stack of magazines, reading and cutting out articles. Or I can skim through a book, learning the major concepts and pulling out quotes I'll be able to use later. And when I'm in town, I maximize my learning time by continually listening to instructive tapes in the car.

Frank A. Clark stated, "Most of us must learn a great deal every day in order to keep ahead of what we forget." Learning something every day is the essence of being a continual learner. You must keep improving yourself, not only acquiring knowledge to replace what you forget or what's out-of-date, but building on what you learned yesterday.

6. DEVELOP A PLAN FOR GROWTH

The key to a life of continual learning and improvement lies in developing a specific plan for growth and following through with it. I recommend a plan that requires an hour a day, five days a week. I use that as the pattern because of a statement by Earl Nightingale, which says, "If a person will spend one hour a day on the same subject for five years, that person will be an expert on that subject." Isn't that an incredible promise? It shows how far we are capable of going when we have the discipline to make growth our daily practice. When I teach leadership conferences, I recommend the following growth plan to participants:

> MONDAY: Spend one hour with a devotional to develop your spiritual life.
> TUESDAY: Spend one hour listening to a leadership podcast or audio lesson.
> WEDNESDAY: Spend one hour filing quotes and reflecting on the content of Tuesday's tape.
> THURSDAY: Spend one hour reading a book on leadership.
> FRIDAY: Spend half the hour reading the book and the other half filing and reflecting.

As you develop your plan for growth, start by identifying the three to five areas in which you desire to grow. Then look for useful materials—books, magazines, audiotapes, videos—and incorporate them into your plan. I recommend that you make it your goal to read twelve books and listen to fifty-two tapes (or read fifty-two articles) each year. Exactly how you go about it doesn't matter, but do it daily. That way you're more likely to follow through and get it done than if you periodically put it off and then try to catch up.

7. PAY THE PRICE

I mentioned before that self-fulfillment focuses on making a person happy, whereas self-development proposes to help a person reach potential. A trade-off of growth is that it is sometimes uncomfortable. It requires discipline. It takes time that you could spend on leisure activities. It costs money to buy materials. You have to face constant change and take risks. And sometimes it's just plain lonely. That's why many people stop growing when the price gets high.

But growth is always worth the price you pay because the alternative is a limited life with unfulfilled potential. Success takes effort, and you can't make the journey if you're sitting back waiting for life to come along and improve you. President Theodore Roosevelt boldly stated, "There has not yet been a person in our history who led a life of ease whose name is worth remembering." Those words were true when he spoke them almost a century ago, and they still apply today.

8. FIND A WAY TO APPLY WHAT YOU LEARN

Jim Rohn urged, "Don't let your learning lead to knowledge. Let your learning lead to action." The bottom line when it comes to personal development is action. If your life doesn't begin to change as a result of what you're learning, you're experiencing one of these problems: You're not giving your growth plan enough time and attention; you're focusing too much time on the wrong areas; or *you're not applying what you learn.*

Successful people develop positive daily habits that help them to grow and learn. One of the things I do to make sure I don't lose what I learn is file it. In my office I have more than twelve hundred files full of articles and information, and I have thousands upon thousands of quotes. But I also make an effort to apply information as soon as I learn it. I do that by asking myself these questions anytime I learn something new:

Where can I use it?
When can I use it?
Who else needs to know it?

These questions take my focus off simply acquiring knowledge and put it onto applying what I learn to my life. Try using them. I think they'll do the same for you.

Author and leadership expert Fred Smith made a statement that summarizes what committing to personal growth is really all about. He said:

> Something in human nature tempts us to stay where we're comfortable. We try to find a plateau, a resting place, where we have comfortable stress and adequate finances. Where we have comfortable associations with people, without the intimidation of meeting new people and entering strange situations.

Of course, all of us need to plateau for a time. We climb and then plateau for assimilation. But once we've assimilated what we've learned, we climb again. It's unfortunate when we've done our last climb. When we have made our last climb, we are old, whether forty or eighty.

Whatever you do, don't allow yourself to stay on a plateau. Commit yourself to climbing the mountain of personal potential—a little at a time—throughout your life. It's one journey you'll never regret having made. According to novelist George Eliot, "It is never too late to be what you might have become."

How Can I Grow
in My Career?

Be better tomorrow than you are today.

A turkey was chatting with a bull. "I would love to be able to get to the top of that tree," sighed the turkey, "but I haven't got the energy."

"Well," replied the bull, "why don't you nibble on some of my droppings? They're packed with nutrients."

The turkey pecked at a lump of dung and found that it actually gave him enough strength to reach the lowest branch of the tree. The next day, after eating some more dung, he reached the second branch. Finally after a fourth night, there he was proudly perched at the top of the tree. But he was promptly spotted by a hunter, who shot him down out of the tree.

The moral of the story: BS might get you to the top, but it won't keep you there.

How Growth Helps You Lead Up

I've met a lot of people who have destination disease. They think that they have "arrived" by obtaining a specific position or getting to a certain level in an organization. When they get to that desired place, they stop striving to grow or improve. What a waste of potential!

There's certainly nothing wrong with the desire to progress in your career, but never try to "arrive." Instead, intend your journey to be open-ended. Most people have no idea how far they can go in life. They aim way too low. I know I did when I first started out, but my life began changing when I stopped setting goals for *where* I wanted to be and started setting the course for *who* I wanted to be. I have discovered for others and me that the key to personal development is being more *growth* oriented than *goal* oriented.

There is no downside to making growth your goal. If you keep learning, you will be better tomorrow than you are today, and that can do so many things for you.

The Better You Are, the More People Listen

If you had an interest in cooking, with whom would you rather spend an hour—Mario Batali (chef, cookbook author, owner of Babbo Ristorante e Enoteca and other restaurants in New York City, and host of two shows on the Food Network) or your neighbor who loves to cook and actually does it "every once in a while"? Or if you were a leadership student, as I am, would you rather spend that hour with the president of the United States or with the person who runs the local convenience store? It's no contest. Why? Because you respect most and can learn best from the person with great competence and experience.

Competence is a key to credibility, and credibility is the key to influencing others. If people respect you, they will listen to you. President Abraham Lincoln said, "I don't think much of a man who is not wiser today than he was yesterday." By focusing on growth, you become wiser each day.

THE BETTER YOU ARE, THE GREATER YOUR VALUE TODAY

If you were to plant fruit and nut trees in your yard, when could you expect to start harvesting from them? Would you be surprised to learn that you had to wait years—three to seven years for fruit, five to fifteen years for nuts? If you want a tree to produce, first you have to let it grow. The more the tree has grown and has created strong roots that can sustain it, the more it can produce. The more it can produce, the greater its value.

People are not all that different. The more they grow, the more valuable they are because they can produce more. In fact, it's said that a tree keeps growing as long as it is living. I would love to live in such a way that the same could be said for me—"he kept growing until the day he died."

I love this quote from Elbert Hubbard: "If what you did yesterday still looks big to you, you haven't done much today." If you look back at past accomplishments, and they don't look small to you now, then you haven't grown very much since you completed them. If you look back at a job you did years ago, and you don't think you could do it better now, then you're not improving in that area of your life.

If you are not continually growing, then it is probably damaging your leadership ability. Warren Bennis and Bert Nanus, authors of *Leaders: The Strategies for Taking Charge*, said, "It is the capacity to develop and improve their skills that distinguishes leaders from followers."[1] If you're not moving forward as a learner, then you are moving backward as a leader.

The Better You Are, the Greater Your Potential for Tomorrow

Who are the hardest people to teach? The people who have never tried to learn. Getting them to accept a new idea is like trying to transplant a tomato plant into concrete. Even if you could get it to go into the ground, you know it isn't going to survive anyway. The more you learn and grow, the greater your capacity to keep learning. And that makes your potential greater and your value for tomorrow higher.

Indian reformer Mahatma Gandhi said, "The difference between what we do and what we are capable of doing would suffice to solve most of the world's problems." That is how great our potential is. All we have to do is keep fighting to learn more, grow more, become more.

One leader I interviewed for this book told me that when he was in his first job, his boss would sit him down after he made a mistake and talk it through with him. Every time before he left one of those meetings, his boss asked, "Did you learn something from this?" and he would ask him to explain. At the time, this young leader thought his boss was being pretty tough on him. But as he progressed through his career, he discovered that many of his successes could be traced back to practices he adopted as a result of those talks. It made a huge positive impact on him because it kept making him better.

If you want to influence the people who are ahead of you in the organization—and keep influencing them—then you need to keep getting better. An investment in your growth is an investment in your ability, your adaptability, and your promotability. No matter how much it costs you to keep growing and learning, the cost of doing nothing is greater.

HOW TO BECOME BETTER TOMORROW

Founding father Ben Franklin said, "By improving yourself, the world is made better. Be not afraid of growing too slowly. Be afraid only of standing still. Forget your mistakes, but remember what they taught you." So how do you become better tomorrow? By becoming better today. The secret of your success can be found in your daily agenda. Here is what I suggest you do to keep growing and leading up:

1. LEARN YOUR CRAFT TODAY

On a wall in the office of a huge tree farm hangs a sign. It says, "The best time to plant a tree is twenty-five years ago. The second best time is today." There is no time like the present to become an expert at your craft. Maybe you wish you had started earlier. Or maybe you wish you had found a better teacher or mentor years ago. None of that matters. Looking back and lamenting will not help you move forward.

A friend of the poet Longfellow asked the secret of his continued interest in life. Pointing to a nearby apple tree, Longfellow said, "The purpose of that apple tree is to grow a little new wood each year. That is what I plan to do." The friend would have found a similar sentiment in one of Longfellow's poems:

> *Not enjoyment and not sorrow*
> *Is our destined end or way;*
> *But to act that each tomorrow*
> *Find us further than today.*[2]

You may not be where you're supposed to be. You may not be what you want to be. You don't have to be what you used to be. And you don't have to ever arrive. You just need to learn to be the best you can be right now. As Napoleon Hill said, "You can't change where you started, but you can change the direction you are going. It's not what you are going to do, but it's what you are doing now that counts."

2. TALK YOUR CRAFT TODAY

Once you reach a degree of proficiency in your craft, then one of the best things you can do for yourself is talk your craft with others on the same and higher levels than you. Many people do this naturally. Guitarists talk about guitars. Parents talk about raising children. Golfers talk about golf. They do so because it's enjoyable, it fuels their passion, it teaches them new skills and insights, and it prepares them to take action.

Talking to peers is wonderful, but if you don't also make an effort to strategically talk your craft with those ahead of you in experience and skill, then you're really missing learning opportunities. Douglas Randlett meets regularly with a group of retired multimillionaires so that he can learn from them. Before he retired, Major League Baseball player Tony Gwynn was known to talk hitting with anybody who had knowledge about it. Every time he saw Ted Williams, they talked hitting.

I enjoy talking about leadership with good leaders all the time. In fact, I make it a point to schedule a learning lunch with someone I admire, at least six times a year. Before I go, I study up on them by reading their books, studying their lessons, listening to their speeches, or whatever else I need to do. My goal is to learn enough about them and their "sweet spot" to ask the right questions. If I do that, then I can learn from their strengths. But that's not my ultimate goal. My goal is to learn what I can transfer from their strength zones to mine. That's where my growth will come from—not from what they're doing. I have to apply what I learn to my situation.

The secret to a great interview is listening. It is the bridge between learning about them and learning about you. And that's your objective.

3. Practice Your Craft Today

William Osler, the physician who wrote *The Principles and Practice of Medicine* in 1892, once told a group of medical students:

> Banish the future. Live only for the hour and its allotted work. Think not of the amount to be accomplished, the difficulties to be overcome, or the end to be attained, but set earnestly at the little task at your elbow, letting

that be sufficient for the day; for surely our plain duty is, as Carlyle says, "Not to see what lies dimly at a distance, but to do what lies clearly at hand."

The only way to improve is to practice your craft until you know it inside and out. At first, you do what you know to do. The more you practice your craft, the more you know. But as you do more, you will also discover more about what you ought to do differently. At that point you have a decision to make: Will you do what you have always done, or will you try to do more of what you think you should do? The only way you improve is to get out of your comfort zone and try new things.

People often ask me, "How can I grow my business?" or, "How can I make my department better?" The answer is for you personally to grow. The only way to grow your organization is to grow the leaders who run it. By making yourself better, you make others better. Retired General Electric CEO Jack Welch said, "Before you are a leader, success is all about growing yourself. When you become a leader, success is all about growing others."[3] And the time to start is today.

3

How Do I Maintain
a Teachable Attitude?

It's what you learn after you know it all that counts.

If you are a highly talented person, you may have a tough time with teachability. Why? Because talented people often think they know it all. And that makes it difficult for them to continually expand their talent. Teachability is not so much about competence and mental capacity as it is about *attitude*. It is the desire to listen, learn, and apply. It is the hunger to discover and grow. It is the willingness to learn, unlearn, and relearn. I love the way Hall of Fame basketball coach John Wooden states it: "It's what you learn after you know it all that counts."

When I teach and mentor leaders, I remind them that if they stop learning, they stop leading. But if they remain teachable and keep learning, they will be able to keep making an impact as leaders. Whatever your talent happens to be—whether it's leadership, craftsmanship, entrepreneurship, or something else—you will expand it if you keep expecting and striving to learn. Talented individuals with teachable attitudes become talent-plus people.

TEACHABILITY TRUTHS

To make the most of your talent and remain teachable, consider the following truths about teaching:

1. NOTHING IS INTERESTING IF YOU ARE NOT INTERESTED

It's a shame when people allow themselves to get in a rut and never climb out. They often miss the best that life has to offer. In contrast, teachable people are fully engaged in life. They get excited about things. They are interested in discovery, discussion, application, and growth. There is a definite relationship between passion and potential.

German philosopher Goethe advised, "Never let a day pass without looking at some perfect work of art, hearing some great piece of music and reading, in part, some great book." The more engaged you are, the more interesting life will be. The more interested you are in exploring and learning, the greater your potential for growth.

2. Successful People View Learning Differently from Those Who Are Unsuccessful

After more than thirty-five years of teaching and training people, I've come to realize that successful people think differently from unsuccessful ones. That doesn't mean that unsuccessful people are unable to think the way successful people do. (In fact, I believe that just about anyone can retrain himself to think differently. That's why I wrote *Thinking for a Change*—to help people learn the thinking skills capable of making them more successful.) Those successful thinking patterns pertain to learning as well.

Teachable people are always open to new ideas and are willing to learn from anyone who has something to offer. American journalist Sydney J. Harris wrote, "A winner knows how much he still has to learn, even when he is considered an expert by others. A loser wants to be considered an expert by others, before he has learned enough to know how little he knows." It's all a matter of attitude.

It's truly remarkable how much a person has to learn before he realizes how little he knows. Back in 1992, I wrote a book called *Developing the Leader Within You*. At the time, I thought, *I've had some success at leadership. I'll write this book, and it will be my contribution to others on this important subject.* I then put *everything* I knew about leadership in that book. But that book was only the beginning. Writing it made me want to learn more about leadership, and my drive to learn went to another level. I searched out more books, lectures, people, and experiences to help me learn. Today, I've written a total of *eight* books on leadership. Am I finished with that topic? No. There are still things to learn—and to teach. My leadership world is expanding, and so am I. The world is vast, and we are so limited. There is much for us to learn—as long as we remain teachable.

3. LEARNING IS MEANT TO BE A LIFELONG PURSUIT

It's said that the Roman scholar Cato started to study Greek when he was more than eighty years old. When asked why he was tackling such a difficult task at his age, he replied, "It is the earliest age I have left." Unlike Cato, too many people regard learning as an event instead of a process. Someone told me that only one-third of all adults read an entire book after their last graduation. Why would that be? Because they view education as a period of life, not a way of life!

Learning is an activity that is not restricted by age. It doesn't matter if you're past eighty, like Cato, or haven't yet entered your teens. Author Julio Melara was only eleven years old when he began to acquire major life lessons that he has been able to carry with him into adulthood and to teach others. Here are some of the things he's learned, taken from his book *It Only Takes Everything You've Got!: Lessons for a Life of Success.*

Here is a list of all the jobs you will not find on my résumé but lessons that have lasted a lifetime:

- Started cutting grass for profit at age 11
  Lesson learned: It is important to give things a clean, professional look.

- Stock clerk at a local food store
  Lesson learned: Making sure that if I am going to sell something, the merchandise needs to be in stock.

- Dishwasher at local restaurant
  Lesson learned: Somebody always has to do the job no one else wants to do. Also, most people have a lot of food on their plates. (They do not finish what they start.)

- A janitor at an office building
  Lesson learned: The importance of cleanliness as it related to image.

- Fry and prep cook at a steak house
  Lesson learned: The importance of preparation and the impact of the right presentation.

- Construction helping hand (lug wood and supplies from one place to another)
  Lesson learned: I do not want to do this for the rest of my life.

- Sold newspaper subscription for daily paper
  Lesson learned: The job of rejection—had to knock on at least thirty doors before I ever sold one subscription.

- Shipping clerk at a plumbing supply house
  Lesson learned: Delivering your project or service on time is just as important as selling it.

- Breakfast cook at a twenty-four-hour restaurant stop
  Lesson learned: How to do fifteen things at once. Also learned about the weird things people like to eat on their eggs.

- Cleaned cars at detailing shop
  Lesson learned: The importance of details (washing vs. detailing). You can pay $15 just to wash the outside of the car or $150 to clean the car inside and out and cover all the details. Details are a pain, but details are valuable.

- Shoe salesman at a retail store
  Lesson learned: To sell customers what they want and like. Also, learned to compliment people and be sincere.

- Busboy at a local diner
  Lesson learned: People enjoy being served with a smile and they love a clean table.

Every stage of life presents lessons to be learned. We can choose to be teachable and continue to learn them, or we can be closed-minded and stop growing. The decision is ours.

4. Pride Is the Number One Hindrance to Teachability

Author, trainer, and speaker Dave Anderson believes

that the number one cause of management failure is pride. He wrote:

> There are many reasons managers fail. For some, the organization outgrows them. Others don't change with the times . . . A few make poor character choices. They look good for a while but eventually discover they can't get out of their own way. Increasingly more keep the wrong people too long because they don't want to admit they made a mistake or have high turnover become a negative reflection on them. Some failures had brilliant past track records but start using their success as a license to build a fence around what they had rather than continue to risk and stretch to build it to even higher levels. But all these causes for management failure have their root in one common cause: pride. In simplest terms, pride is devastating . . . the pride that inflates your sense of self-worth and distorts your perspective of reality.

While envy is the deadly sin that comes from feelings of *inferiority*, the deadly sin of pride comes from feelings of *superiority*. It creates an arrogance of success, an inflated sense of self-worth accompanied by a distorted perspective of reality.

Such an attitude leads to a loss of desire to learn and an unwillingness to change. It makes a person unteachable.

How to Take Your Talent to the Next Level

If you want to expand your talent, you must become teachable. That is the pathway to growth. Futurist and author John Naisbitt believes that "the most important skill to acquire is learning how to learn." Here is what I suggest as you pursue teachability and become a talent-plus person:

1. Learn to Listen

The first step in teachability is learning to listen. American writer and philosopher Henry David Thoreau wrote, "It takes two to speak the truth—one to speak and one to hear." Being a good listener helps us to know people better, to learn what they have learned, and to show them that we value them as individuals.

As you go through each day, remember that you can't learn if you're always talking. As the old saying goes, "There's a reason you have one mouth but two ears." Listen to others, remain humble, and you will begin to learn things every day that can help you expand your talent.

2. UNDERSTAND THE LEARNING PROCESS

Here's how the learning typically works:

STEP 1: Act.
STEP 2: Look for your mistakes and evaluate.
STEP 3: Search for a way to do it better.
STEP 4: Go back to step 1.

Remember, the greatest enemy of learning is knowing, and the goal of all learning is action, not knowledge. If what you are doing does not in some way contribute to what you or others are doing in life, then question its value and be prepared to make changes.

3. LOOK FOR AND PLAN TEACHABLE MOMENTS

If you look for opportunities to learn in every situation, you will become a talent-plus person and expand your talent to its potential. But you can also take another step beyond that and actively seek out and plan teachable moments. You can do that by reading books, visiting places that will inspire you, attending events that will prompt you to pursue change, listening to lessons, and spending time with people who will stretch you and expose you to new experiences.

I've had the privilege to spend time with many remarkable people, and the natural reward has been the opportunity to learn. In my personal relationships, I've also gravitated toward people from whom I can learn. My closest friends are people who challenge my thinking—and often change it. They lift me up in many ways. And I've found that I often live out something stated by Spanish philosopher and writer Baltasar Gracian: "Make your friends your teachers and mingle the pleasures of conversation with the advantages of instruction." You can do the same. Cultivate friendships with people who challenge and add value to you, and try to do the same for them. It will change your life.

4. Make Your Teachable Moments Count

Even people who are strategic about seeking teachable moments can miss the whole point of the experience. I say this because for thirty years I've been a speaker at conferences and workshops—events that are designed to help people learn. But I've found that many people walk away from an event and do very little with what they heard after closing their notebooks. It would be like a jewelry designer going to a gem merchant to buy fine gems, placing them carefully into a case, and then putting that case on the shelf to collect dust. What's the value of acquiring the gems if they're never going to be used?

We tend to focus on learning events instead of the learning process. Because of this, I try to help people take action steps that will help them implement what they learn. I suggest that in their notes, they use a code to mark things that jump out at them:

T indicates you need to some time thinking on
    that point.
C indicates something you need to change.
J A smiley face means you are doing that thing
    particularly well.
A indicates something you need to apply.
S means you need to share that information with
    someone else.

After the conference I recommend that they create to-do lists based on what they marked, then schedule time to follow through.

5. Ask Yourself, "Am I Really Teachable?"

I've said it before, but it bears repeating: all the good advice in the world won't help if you don't have a teachable spirit. To know whether you are *really* open to new ideas and new ways of doing things, answer the following questions:

1. Am I open to other people's ideas?
2. Do I listen more than I talk?
3. Am I open to changing my opinion based on new information?
4. Do I readily admit when I am wrong?
5. Do I observe before acting on a situation?
6. Do I ask questions?
7. Am I willing to ask a question that will expose my ignorance?
8. Am I open to doing things in a way I haven't done before?
9. Am I willing to ask for directions?
10. Do I act defensive when criticized, or do I listen openly for the truth?

If you answered no to one or more of these questions, then you have room to grow in the area of teachability. You need to soften your attitude and learn humility, and remember the words of John Wooden: "Everything we know we learned from someone else!"

Thomas Edison was the guest of the governor of North Carolina when the politician complimented him on his creative genius.

"I am not a great inventor," countered Edison.

"But you have more than a thousand patents to your credit," the governor stated.

"Yes, but about the only invention I can really claim as absolutely original is the phonograph," Edison replied.

"I'm afraid I don't understand what you mean," the governor remarked.

"Well," explained Edison, "I guess I'm an awfully good sponge. I absorb ideas from every course I can, and put them to practical use. Then I improve them until they become of some value. The ideas which I use are mostly the ideas of other people who don't develop them themselves."

What a remarkable description of someone who used teachability to expand his talent! That is what a talent-plus person does. That is what all of us should strive to do.

4

WHAT ROLE DO OTHERS
PLAY IN MY GROWTH?

What kind of attitude do you have when it comes to learning from others? All people fall into one of the categories described by the following statements:

NO ONE CAN TEACH ME ANYTHING—
ARROGANT ATTITUDE

I think we sometimes assume that ignorance is the greatest enemy of teachability. However, that really has little to do with teachability. Haven't you known some highly educated and highly successful people who do not want to hear the suggestions or opinions of anyone else? Some people think they know it all! A person who creates a large, successful organization may think he can't learn from people who run a smaller one. A person who receives a doctorate can become unreceptive to instruction from anyone else because she is now considered an expert. Another person who is the most experienced in a company or department may not listen to the ideas of someone younger.

Such people don't realize how much they are hurting themselves. The reality is that no one is too old, too smart, or too successful to learn something new. The only thing that can come between a person and the ability to learn and improve is a bad attitude.

SOMEONE CAN TEACH ME EVERYTHING— NAIVE ATTITUDE

People who realize that they have room to grow often seek a mentor. That's usually a good thing. However, it's naive for individuals to think they can learn everything they need to know from just one person. People don't need *a* mentor—they need *many* mentors. I've learned so much from so many people. Les Stobbe taught me how to write. My brother, Larry, is my business mentor. I've learned a lot about communication from Andy Stanley. Tom Mullins models relationships for me. If I tried to include all the people who have taught me over the years, I'd fill page after page with names.

Everyone Can Teach Me Something—
Teachable Attitude

The people who learn the most aren't necessarily the ones who spend time with the smartest people. They are the ones with a teachable attitude. Every person has something to share—a lesson learned, an observation, a life experience. We just need to be willing to listen. In fact, often people teach us things when they don't intend to do so. Ask any parents and you will find out that they learned things from their children—even when their kids were infants incapable of communicating a single word. The only time people can't teach us things is when we are unwilling to learn.

I'm not saying that every person you meet *will* teach you something. All I'm saying is that people have the potential to do so—if you'll let them.

How to Learn from Others

If you have a teachable attitude—or you are willing to adopt one—you will be positioned well to learn from others. Then all you will need to do is take the following five steps:

1. MAKE LEARNING YOUR PASSION

Management expert Philip B. Crosby noted:

There is a theory of human behavior that says people subconsciously retard their own intellectual growth. They come to rely on clichés and habits. Once they reach the age of their own personal comfort with the world, they stop learning and their mind runs on idle for the rest of their days. They may progress organizationally, they may be ambitious and eager, and they may even work night and day. But they learn no more.[1]

That's sometimes the problem with people who received the *positions* they dreamed of or reached the *goals* they set for their organizations or earned the *degrees* they strived for. In their minds, they have reached their destinations. They get comfortable.

If you desire to keep growing, you cannot sit back in a comfort zone. You need to make learning your goal. Do that and you will never run out of gas mentally, and your motivation will be strong. And don't worry about having people to teach you. Greek philosopher Plato said, "When the pupil is ready, the teacher will appear."

2. Value People

In 1976, I had been in my career for seven years, and I felt successful. In those days, churches were often judged by the success of their Sunday school programs, and the church I led had the fastest-growing program in the state of Ohio. And by then my church had grown to be the largest in my denomination. But I still wanted to learn. That year I signed up to attend a conference. There were three speakers that I wanted to hear. They were older, more successful, and more experienced than I was.

During the conference, one of the sessions was an idea exchange where anybody could talk. I figured it would be a waste of time, and I was going to skip it, but my curiosity got the best of me. It turned out to be a real eye-opener. Person after person shared what was working in his organization, and I sat there scribbling notes and jotting down ideas. It turned out that I learned more during that session than in all the others combined.

That surprised me, and later I realized why. Before that conference, I thought only older, more successful people could teach me anything. I had walked into that room placing very little value on the other people there. And that was a wrong attitude. People don't learn from people they don't value. I determined to change my thinking from that day forward.

3. DEVELOP RELATIONSHIPS WITH GROWTH POTENTIAL

It's true that everyone has *something* to teach us, but that doesn't mean anyone can teach us *everything* we want to learn. We need to find people who are especially likely to help us grow—experts in our field, creative thinkers who will stretch us mentally, achievers who will inspire us to go to the next level. Learning is often the reward for spending time with remarkable people. Who they are and what they know rub off. As Donald Clifton and Paula Nelson, authors of *Soar with Your Strengths*, observe, "Relationships help us define who we are and what we become."

4. IDENTIFY PEOPLE'S UNIQUENESS AND STRENGTHS

Philosopher-poet Ralph Waldo Emerson remarked, "I have never met a man who was not my superior in some particular." People grow best in their areas of strength—and can learn the most from another person's area of strength. For that reason, you can't be indiscriminate in choosing the people you seek out to teach you.

In the mid-1970s, I identified the top ten church leaders in the nation, and I tried to get an appointment for lunch with each of them. I even offered them one hundred dollars for an hour of their time—that was a half week's pay back then. Some were willing to meet me. Others weren't. I was extremely grateful to the ones who did.

My wife and I didn't have much money then, and these leaders lived all over the country, so we planned our vacations for several years around these visits. Why would I go to such lengths to meet these people? Because I was dying to learn the unique skills and strengths they possessed. The meetings made a huge difference in my life. And do you know what? Connection with great men and women continues to affect my life. Every month I try to meet with someone I admire and from whom I want to learn.

5. Ask Questions

The first year I was in college, I took a part-time job at a locker plant in Circleville, Ohio. It was a place where cows were slaughtered and the meat was stored in giant refrigerated lockers. My job was to haul freshly processed meat to the refrigeration areas and to retrieve orders of meat for customers.

Anytime I'm exposed to something new—and this was a new area for me—I try to learn about it. And the best way to learn is to watch and ask questions. I had been working for about two weeks when Pense, an old guy who had worked there for years, pulled me aside and said, "Son, let me tell you something. You ask too many questions. I've been working here for a long time. I kill cows. That's all I do—and that's all I'm gonna do. The more you know, the more they expect you to do." I had a hard time understanding why anybody *wouldn't* want to learn and grow. But obviously he was committed not to change.

Writer Johann Wolfgang von Goethe believed that "one ought, every day at least, to hear a little song, read a good poem, see a fine picture, and, if it were possible, to speak a few reasonable words." I would add that one ought to also ask questions to learn something new each day. The person who asks the right questions learns the most.

Choose a Mentor to Help You Grow

You must have the right attitude toward others in order to grow. But if you really want to maximize your progress, you need to take another step. You need to find a mentor who can model what you want to learn and help you grow. At first it doesn't have to be someone you know. Start by reading books, watching videos, and attending conferences. Read blogs. Then start looking for someone who can help you go to the next level.

Give careful thought to the people you follow because they will impact the course of your life. I have developed six questions to ask myself before picking a model to follow. Perhaps they will help you when choosing a mentor.

DOES MY MODEL'S LIFE DESERVE A FOLLOWING?

This question relates to quality of character. If the answer is not a clear yes, I have to be very careful. I will become like the people I follow, and I don't want models with flawed character.

DOES MY MODEL'S LIFE HAVE A FOLLOWING?

This question looks at credibility. It is possible to be the very first person to discover a leader worth following, but it doesn't happen very often. If the person has no following, he or she may not be worth following.

If my answer to either of the first two questions is no, I

don't have to bother with the other four. I need to look for another model.

What Is the Main Strength That Influences Others to Follow My Model?

What does the model have to offer me? What is his best? Also note that strong leaders have weaknesses as well as strengths. I don't want to inadvertently emulate the weaknesses.

Does My Model Produce Other Leaders?

The answer to this question will tell me whether the model's leadership priorities match mine in regard to developing new leaders.

Is My Model's Strength Reproducible in My Life?

If I can't reproduce his strength in my life, his modeling will not benefit me. For instance, if you admire Shaquille O'Neil's ability as a basketball center, but you're only 5 feet, 9 inches tall and weigh 170 pounds, you are not going to be able to reproduce his strengths. Find appropriate models . . .

but strive for improvement. Don't be too quick to say that a strength is not reproducible. Most are. Don't limit your potential.

IF MY MODEL'S STRENGTH IS REPRODUCIBLE IN MY LIFE, WHAT STEPS MUST I TAKE TO DEVELOP AND DEMONSTRATE THAT STRENGTH?

You must develop a plan of action. If you only answer the questions and never implement a plan to develop those strengths in yourself, you are only performing an intellectual exercise.

The models we choose may or may not be accessible to us in a personal way. Some may be national figures, such as a president. Or they may be people from history. They can certainly benefit you, but not the way a personal mentor can.

GUIDELINES FOR MENTORING RELATIONSHIPS

When you find someone who can personally mentor you, use these guidelines to help develop a positive mentoring relationship with that person:

CLARIFY YOUR LEVEL OF EXPECTATIONS

Generally, the goal of mentoring is improvement, not perfection. Perhaps only a few people can be truly excellent—but all of us can become better.

ACCEPT A SUBORDINATE, LEARNING POSITION

Don't let ego get in the way of learning. Trying to impress the mentor with your knowledge or ability will set up a mental barrier between you. It will prevent you from receiving what he is giving. Be humble and patient.

RESPECT THE MENTOR, BUT DON'T IDOLIZE HIM

Respect allows us to accept what the mentor is teaching. But making the mentor an idol removes the ability to be objective and critical—faculties we need for adapting a mentor's knowledge and experience to ourselves. Learn from your mentor's weaknesses as well as strengths.

IMMEDIATELY PUT INTO EFFECT WHAT YOU ARE LEARNING

In the best mentoring relationships, what is learned comes quickly into focus. As soon as you learn something new, put it into practice or teach it to someone else. You will assimilate it more quickly if you do.

BE DISCIPLINED IN RELATING TO THE MENTOR

Arrange for ample and consistent time, select the subject matter in advance, and do your homework to make the sessions profitable.

REWARD YOUR MENTOR WITH YOUR OWN PROGRESS

If you show appreciation but make no progress, the mentor experiences failure. Your progress is his highest reward. Strive for growth, then communicate your progress.

DON'T THREATEN TO GIVE UP

Let your mentor know you have made a decision for progress and that you are a persistent person—a determined winner. Then he will know he is not wasting his time.

There is no substitute for your own personal growth. If you are not receiving and growing, you will not be able to give to the people you nurture and develop.

Part II

The Ongoing Process
of Improvement

5

WHERE SHOULD I FOCUS
MY TIME AND ENERGY?

To reach your potential, get in your strength zone.

Can you remember the first lesson you ever learned about leadership? I can. It came from my dad. He used to tell my brother, my sister, and me, "Find out what you do well and keep on doing it." That wasn't just casual advice. He and my mother made it their mission to help us discover our strengths and start developing them before we were old enough to leave home and go out on our own.

Dad also reinforced that advice by living it. One of his favorite sayings was "This one thing I do." He had an uncanny ability to remain focused within his areas of strength. That, coupled with his determination to finish what he started, served him well throughout his career and beyond. He stays in his strength zone. It is one of the reasons he has always been the greatest inspiration for my life.

SEARCHING FOR STRENGTHS

When I started my career, I was committed to finding my strength zone and working to stay in it. However, I was frustrated for my first few years working. Like many inexperienced leaders, I tried to do many different things to discover what I really could do well. In addition, people's expectations for what I would do and how I would lead did not always match my strengths. I think that is true for many young leaders just starting out.

My responsibilities and obligations sometimes required that I perform tasks for which I possessed neither talent nor skill. I was often ineffective as a result. It took me several years to sort all this out, find my strength zone, and recruit and develop other people to compensate for my weaknesses.

If you are a young leader and you are still uncertain about where your strengths lie, don't get discouraged. Try to be patient and keep working hard. If you persevere you will figure it out. Here's what I know: no matter if you're just starting out or if you are at the peak of your career, the more you work in your strength zone, the more successful you will be.

DEFINING PERSONAL SUCCESS

I've heard many definitions of success from many people over the years. In fact, I've embraced different definitions myself at different stages of my life. But in the last fifteen years, I have zeroed in on a definition that I think captures success no matter who people are or what they want to do. I believe success is

Knowing your purpose in life,
Growing to your maximum potential, and
Sowing seeds that benefit others.

If you are able to do those three things, you are successful. However, none of them is possible unless you find and stay in your strength zone.

I love the story of a group of neighborhood boys who built a tree house and formed their own club. When the grown-ups were told who had been selected for which office, they were astonished to hear that a four-year-old had been elected president.

"That boy must be a born leader," one dad observed. "How did it happen that all you bigger boys voted for him?"

"Well, you see, Dad," his son replied, "he can't very well be secretary because he doesn't know how to read or write. He couldn't be treasurer, because he can't count. He would never do for sergeant at arms because he's too little to throw anybody out. If we didn't choose him for anything, he'd feel bad. So we made him president."

Real life, of course, doesn't work that way. You don't become an effective leader by default. You must be intentional. And you must work from your strengths.

Whenever I mentor people and help them discover their purpose, I always encourage them to start the process by discovering their strengths, not exploring their shortcomings. Why? Because people's purpose in life is always connected to their giftedness. It always works that way. You are not called to do something that you have no talent for. You will discover your purpose by finding and remaining in your strength zone.

Similarly, you cannot grow to your maximum potential if you continually work outside of your strength zone. Improvement is always related to ability. The greater your natural ability, the greater your potential for improvement. I've known people who thought that reaching their potential would come from shoring up their weaknesses. But do you know what happens when you spend all your time working on your weaknesses and never developing your strengths? If you work really hard, you might claw your way all the way up to mediocrity! But you'll never get beyond it.

The final piece of the puzzle—living a life that benefits others—always depends upon us giving our best, not our worst. You can't change the world by giving only leftovers or by performing with mediocrity. Only your best will add value to others and lift them up.

FINDING YOUR OWN STRENGTH ZONE

British poet and lexicographer Samuel Johnson said, "Almost every man wastes part of his life in attempts to display qualities which he does not possess." If you have an image in your mind of what talents people are supposed to have, yet you do not possess them, then you will have a difficult time finding your true strengths. You need to discover and develop who *you* are. Here are a few suggestions to help you:

1. ASK, "WHAT AM I DOING WELL?"

People who reach their potential spend less time asking, "What am I doing right?" and more time asking, "What am

I doing well?" The first is a moral question; the second is a talent question. You should always strive to do what's right. But doing what's right doesn't tell you anything about your talent.

2. GET SPECIFIC

When we consider our strengths, we tend to think too broadly. Peter Drucker, the father of modern management, wrote, "The great mystery isn't that people do things badly but that they occasionally do a few things well. The only thing that is universal is incompetence. Strength is always specific! Nobody ever commented, for example, that the great violinist Jascha Heifetz probably couldn't play the trumpet well." The more specific you can get about your strengths, the better the chance you can find your "sweet spot." Why be on the fringes of your strength zone when you have a chance to be right in the center?

3. LISTEN FOR WHAT OTHERS PRAISE

Many times we take our talents for granted. We think because we can do something well, anyone can. Often that's not true. How can you tell when you're overlooking a skill or talent? Listen to what others say. Your strengths will capture the attention of others and draw them to you. On the other hand, when you're working in areas of weakness, few people will show interest. If others are continually praising you in a particular area, start developing it.

4. CHECK OUT THE COMPETITION

You don't want to spend all your time comparing yourself to others; that's not healthy. But you don't want to waste your time doing something that others do much better. Former GE CEO Jack Welch asserts, "If you don't have a competitive advantage, don't compete." People don't pay for average. If you don't have the talent to do something better than the competition, place your focus elsewhere.

To get a better picture of where you stand in relationship to the competition, you need to ask yourself the following questions:

- Are others doing what I am doing?
- Are they doing it well?
- Are they doing it better than I am?
- Can I become better than they are?
- If I do become better, what will be the result?
- If I don't become better, what will be the result?

The answer to the last question is: you lose. Why? Because your competition is working in their strength zone and you aren't!

The point of asking yourself these questions is not for you to try to be like others. It's to help you see where you are different from others. Former all-star baseball catcher Jim Sundberg advised, "Discover your uniqueness, then discipline yourself to develop it." That's what I've tried to do. Many years ago I realized that one of my strengths was communicating. People have always been motivated when they hear me speak. After a while, many opportunities were given to me to speak at events with other motivational speakers. At first it was very intimidating because they were so good. But as I listened to them, the thing I kept asking myself was, "What can I do that will set me apart from them?" I felt it might not be possible for me to be better than they were, but it would be possible for me to be different. Over time I discovered and developed that difference. I would strive to be a motivational *teacher*, not just a motivation *speaker*. I wanted people not only to enjoy what I shared but to also be able to apply what I taught to their lives. For more than two decades, I have disciplined my life to develop that uniqueness. It's my niche— my strength zone.

To Be a Successful Leader, Find and Develop the Strength Zones of Your People

Whenever you see people who are successful in their work, you can rest assured that they are working in their strength zone. But that's not enough if you want to be successful as a leader. Good leaders help others find their strength zones and empower them to work in them. In fact, the best leaders are characterized by the ability to recognize the special abilities and limitations of others, and the capacity to fit their people into the jobs where they will do best.

Sadly, most people are not working in their areas of strength and therefore are not reaching their potential. The Gallup organization conducted research on 1.7 million people in the workplace. According to their findings, only 20 percent of employees feel that their strengths are in play every day in the work setting.[1] In my opinion, that is largely the fault of their leaders. They have failed to help their people find their strengths and place them in the organization where their strengths can be an asset to the company.

In her book *Hesselbein on Leadership*, Frances Hesselbein, the chairman of the board of governors of the Leader to Leader Institute founded by Peter F. Drucker, wrote, "Peter

Drucker reminds us that organizations exist to make people's strengths effective and their weaknesses irrelevant. And this is the work of effective leaders. Drucker also tells us that there may be born leaders but there are far too few to depend on them."

If you desire to be an effective leader, you must develop the ability to develop people in their areas of strength. How do you do that?

STUDY AND KNOW THE PEOPLE ON YOUR TEAM

What are your people's strengths and weaknesses? Whom do they relate to on the team? Are they growing and do they have more growth potential in the area in which they're working? Is their attitude an asset or a liability? Do they love what they do and are they doing it well? These are questions that must be answered by the leader.

COMMUNICATE TO INDIVIDUALS HOW THEY FIT ON THE TEAM

What are the strengths that they bring to the table? Are there times their contribution will be especially valuable? How do they complement the other members of the team? What do they need from the other players that will complement their weaknesses? The more that people know how they fit on a team, the more they will desire to properly make the most of their fit and maximize their contribution.

COMMUNICATE TO ALL TEAM MEMBERS HOW EACH PLAYER FITS ON THE TEAM

It's obvious that you can't have a winning team without teamwork. However, not every leader takes steps to help team members work together. If you communicate to all the players how all the people fit together and what strengths they bring for their role, then teammates will value and respect one another.

EMPHASIZE COMPLETING ONE ANOTHER ABOVE COMPETING WITH ONE ANOTHER

Healthy competition between teammates is good. It presses them to do their best. But in the end, team members need to work together for the sake of the team, not only for themselves.

To some leaders, the idea of focusing almost entirely on strengths seems counterintuitive. Several years ago I was spending a day with leaders of several companies, and one of the subjects I addressed was the importance of staying in your strength zone. I repeatedly encouraged them not to work with their areas of weakness related to ability. During the Q&A session, a CEO pushed back against the idea. The example he used was that of Tiger Woods.

"When Tiger plays a bad round of golf," he observed, "he goes straight to the driving range and practices for hours. You see, John, he's working on his weaknesses."

"No," I replied, "he's working on his strengths. Tiger is the greatest golfer in the world. He's practicing golf shots. He's not practicing accounting or music or basketball. He is working on a weakness within his strength zone. That will always produce positive results."

Working on a weakness in your strength zone will always produce greater results than working on a strength in a weak area. I love golf, but if I practice golf shots, I will never greatly improve. Why? Because I'm an average golfer. Practice won't make perfect—it will make permanent! If I want to make progress, I need to keep working on my leadership and communication. Those are my strength zones.

Where are yours? If you're spending time in them, then you are making an investment in your success.

6

HOW DO I OVERCOME OBSTACLES
TO SELF-IMPROVEMENT?

Grasp the positive benefits of negative experiences.

Working artists David Bayles and Ted Orland tell a story about an art teacher who did an experiment with his grading system for two groups of students. It is a parable on the benefits of failure. Here is what happened:

The ceramics teacher announced on opening day that he was dividing the class into two groups. All those on the left side of the studio, he said, would be graded solely on the *quantity* of work they produced, all those on the right solely on its *quality*. His procedure was simple: on the final day of class he would bring in his bathroom scales and weigh the work of the "quantity" group: fifty pounds of pots rated an "A," forty pounds a "B," and so on. Those being graded on "quality," however, needed to produce only one pot—albeit a perfect one—to get an "A." Well, came grading time and a curious fact emerged: the works of the highest quality were all produced by the group being graded for quantity. It seems that while the "quantity" group was busily churning out piles of work—and learning from their mistakes—the "quality" group had sat theorizing about perfection, and in the end had little more to show for their efforts than grandiose theories and a pile of dead clay.[1]

It doesn't matter whether your objectives are in the area of art, business, ministry, sports, or relationships. The only way you can get ahead is to fail early, fail often, and fail forward.

TAKE THE JOURNEY

I teach leadership to thousands of people each year at numerous conferences. And one of my deepest concerns is always that some people will go home from the event and nothing will change in their lives. They enjoy the "show" but fail to implement any of the ideas presented to them. I tell people continually: We overestimate the event and underestimate the process. Every fulfilled dream occurred because of dedication to a process. (That's one of the reasons I write books and create programs on audiocassette—so that people can engage in the ongoing *process* of growth.)

People naturally tend toward inertia. That's why self-improvement is such a struggle. But that's also why adversity lies at the heart of every success. The process of achievement comes through repeated failures and the constant struggle to climb to a higher level.

Most people will grudgingly concede that they must make it through some adversity in order to succeed. They'll acknowledge that they have to experience the occasional setback to make progress. But I believe that success comes only if you take that thought one step farther. To achieve your dreams, you must *embrace* adversity and make failure a regular part of your life. If you're not failing, you're probably not really moving forward.

THE BENEFITS OF ADVERSITY

Psychologist Dr. Joyce Brothers asserts, "The person interested in success has to learn to view failure as a healthy, inevitable part of the process of getting to the top." Adversity and the failure that often results from it should be expected in the process of succeeding, and they should be viewed as absolutely critical parts of it. In fact, the benefits of adversity are many. Consider these reasons to embrace adversity and persevere through it:

1. ADVERSITY CREATES RESILIENCE

Nothing in life breeds resilience like adversity and failure. A study in *Time* magazine in the mid-1980s described the incredible resilience of a group of people who had lost their jobs three times because of plant closings. Psychologists expected them to be discouraged, but they were surprisingly optimistic. Their adversity had actually created an advantage. Because they had already lost a job and found a new one at least twice, they were better able to handle adversity than people who had worked for only one company and found themselves unemployed.[2]

2. ADVERSITY DEVELOPS MATURITY

Adversity can make you better if you don't let it make you bitter. Why? Because it promotes wisdom and maturity. American playwright William Saroyan spoke to this issue:

"Good people are good because they've come to wisdom through failure. We get very little wisdom from success, you know."

As the world continues to change at a faster and faster rate, maturity with flexibility becomes increasingly important. These qualities come from weathering difficulties. Harvard business school professor John Kotter says, "I can imagine a group of executives 20 years ago discussing a candidate for a top job and saying, 'This guy had a big failure when he was 32.' Everyone else would say, 'Yep, yep, that's a bad sign.' I can imagine that same group considering a candidate today and saying, 'What worries me about this guy is that he's never failed.'"[3] The problems we face and overcome prepare our hearts for future difficulties.

3. Adversity Pushes the Envelope of Accepted Performance

Lloyd Ogilvie told of a friend who was a circus performer in his youth. The fellow described learning to work on the trapeze:

> Once you know that the net below will catch you, you
> stop worrying about falling. You actually learn to fall

successfully! What that means is, you can concentrate on catching the trapeze swinging toward you, and not on falling, because repeated falls in the past have convinced you that the net is strong and reliable when you do fall . . . The result of falling and being caught by the net is a mysterious confidence and daring on the trapeze. You fall less. Each fall makes you able to risk more.[4]

Until a person learns from experience that he can live through adversity, he is reluctant to buck mindless tradition, push the envelope of organizational performance, or challenge himself to press his physical limits. Failure prompts a person to rethink the status quo.

4. ADVERSITY PROVIDES GREATER OPPORTUNITIES

I believe that eliminating problems limits our potential. Just about every successful entrepreneur I've met has numerous stories of adversity and setbacks that opened doors to greater opportunity. For example, in 1978, Bernie Marcus, the son of a poor Russian cabinetmaker in Newark, New Jersey, was fired from Handy Dan, a do-it-yourself hardware retailer. That prompted Marcus to team with Arthur Blank to start their own business. In 1979, they opened their first store in Atlanta, Georgia. It was called The Home Depot. Today, The Home Depot has more than 760 stores employing more than 157,000 people, the business has expanded to include overseas operations, and each year the corporation does more than $30 billion in sales.

I'm sure Bernie Marcus wasn't very happy about getting fired from his job at Handy Dan. But if he hadn't been, who knows whether he would have achieved the success he has today.

5. Adversity Prompts Innovation

Early in the twentieth century, a boy whose family had immigrated from Sweden to Illinois sent twenty-five cents to a publisher for a book on photography. What he received instead was a book on ventriloquism. What did he do? He adapted and learned ventriloquism. The boy was Edgar Bergen, and for more than forty years he entertained audiences with the help of a wooden dummy named Charlie McCarthy.

The ability to innovate is at the heart of creativity—a vital component in success. University of Houston professor Jack Matson recognized that fact and developed a course that his students came to call "Failure 101." In it, Matson assigns students to build mock-ups of products that no one would ever buy. His goal is to get students to equate failure with innovation instead of defeat. That way they will free themselves to try new things. "They learn to reload and get ready to shoot again," says Matson. If you want to succeed, you have to learn to make adjustments to the way you do things and try again. Adversity helps to develop that ability.

6. ADVERSITY RECAPS UNEXPECTED BENEFITS

The average person makes a mistake and automatically thinks that it's a failure. But some of the greatest stories of success can be found in the unexpected benefits of mistakes. For example, most people are familiar with the story of Edison and the phonograph: he discovered it while trying to invent something entirely different. But did you know that Kellogg's Corn Flakes resulted when boiled wheat was left in a baking pan overnight? Or that Ivory soap floats because a batch was left in the mixer too long and had a large volume of air whipped into it? Or that Scott Towels were launched when a toilet paper machine put too many layers of tissue together?

Horace Walpole said that "in science, mistakes always precede the truth." That's what happened to German-Swiss chemist Christian Friedrich Schönbein. One day he was working in the kitchen—which his wife had strictly forbidden—and was experimenting with sulfuric acid and nitric acid. When he accidentally spilled some of the mixture on the kitchen table, he thought he was in trouble. (He *knew* he would experience "adversity" when his wife found out!) He hurriedly snatched up a cotton apron, wiped up the mess, and hung the apron by the fire to dry.

Suddenly there was a violent explosion. Evidently the cellulose in the cotton underwent a process called *nitration*. Unwittingly Schönbein had invented nitrocellulose—what came to be called smokeless gunpowder or guncotton. He went on to market his invention, which made him a lot of money.

7. Adversity Motivates

Years ago, when Bear Bryant was coaching the University of Alabama's football team, the Crimson Tide was ahead by only six points in a game with less than two minutes remaining in the fourth quarter. Bryant sent his quarterback into the game with instructions to play it safe and run out the clock.

In the huddle, the quarterback said, "Coach says to play it safe, but that's what they're expecting. Let's give them a surprise." And with that, he called a pass play.

When the quarterback dropped back and threw the pass, the defending cornerback, who was a champion sprinter, intercepted the ball and headed toward the end zone, expecting to score a touchdown. The quarterback, who was not known as a good runner, took off after the cornerback and ran him down from behind, tackling him on the 5-yard line. His effort saved the game.

After the clock ran out, the opposing coach approached Bear Bryant and said, "What's this business about your quarterback not being a runner? He ran down my speedster from behind!"

Bryant responded, "Your man was running for six points. My man was running for his life."

Nothing can motivate a person like adversity. Olympic diver Pat McCormick discusses this point: "I think failure is one of the great motivators. After my narrow loss in the 1948 trials, I knew how really good I could be. It was the defeat that focused all my concentration on my training and goals." McCormick went on to win two gold medals in the Olympics in Helsinki in 1952 and another two in Melbourne four years later.

If you can step back from the negative circumstances facing you, you will be able to discover their positive benefits. That is almost always true; you simply have to be willing to look for them—and not take the adversity you are experiencing too personally.

If you lose your job, think about the resilience you're developing. If you try something daring and survive, evaluate what you learned about yourself—and how it will help you take on new challenges. If a bookstore gets your order wrong, figure out whether it's an opportunity to learn a new skill. And if you experience a train wreck in your career, think of the maturity it's developing in you. Besides, Bill Vaughan maintains that "in the game of life it's a good idea to have a few early losses, which relieves you of the pressure of trying to maintain an undefeated season." Always measure an obstacle next to the size of the dream you're pursuing. It's all in how you look at it.

WHAT COULD BE WORSE?

One of the most incredible stories of adversity overcome and success gained is that of Joseph, who was an ancient Hebrew. You may be familiar with the story. He was born the eleventh of twelve sons in a wealthy Middle Eastern family whose trade was raising livestock. As a teenager, Joseph alienated his brothers. First, he was his father's favorite, even though he was nearly the youngest. Second, he used to tell his father anytime his brothers weren't doing their work properly with the sheep. And third, he made the mistake of telling his older brothers that one day he would be in charge of them. Some of his brothers wanted to kill him, but the eldest, Reuben, prevented them from doing that. So when Reuben wasn't around, the others sold him into slavery.

Joseph ended up in Egypt working in the house of the captain of the guard, a man named Potiphar. Because of his leadership and administrative skills, Joseph quickly rose in the ranks, and before long, he was running the entire household. He was making the best of a bad situation. But then things got worse. The wife of his master tried to persuade him to sleep with her. When he refused, she accused *him* of making advances to *her* and got Potiphar to throw Joseph in prison.

From Slavery to Prison

At that point, Joseph was in a really difficult position. He was separated from his family. He was living in a foreign land. He was a slave. And he was locked in prison. But again, he made the best of a tough situation. Before long, the warden of the prison put Joseph in charge of all prisoners and the prison's daily activities.

Joseph met a fellow prisoner who had been an official in Pharaoh's court, the chief cupbearer. And Joseph was able to do him a favor by interpreting the man's dream. When he saw that the official was grateful, Joseph made a request of him in return.

"When all goes well with you," Joseph asked, "remember me and show me kindness; mention me to Pharaoh and get me out of this prison. For I was forcibly carried off from the land of the Hebrews, and even here I have done nothing to deserve being put in a dungeon."[5]

Joseph had hope a few days later when the official was returned to court and the good graces of the monarch. He expected any minute to receive word that Pharaoh was setting him free. But he waited. And waited. Two *years* passed before the cupbearer remembered Joseph, and he did so only because Pharaoh wanted someone to interpret his dreams.

FINALLY THE PAYOFF

In the end, Joseph was able to interpret Pharaoh's dreams. And because the Hebrew showed such wisdom, the Egyptian ruler put Joseph in charge of the entire kingdom. As the result of Joseph's leadership, planning, and system of food storage, when famine struck the Middle East seven years later, many thousands of people who otherwise would have died were able to survive, including Joseph's own family. When his brothers traveled to Egypt for relief from the famine—*twenty* years after selling him into slavery—they discovered that their brother Joseph was not only alive, but second in command of the most powerful kingdom in the world.

Few people would welcome the adversity of thirteen years in bondage as a slave and prisoner. But as far as we know, Joseph never gave up hope and never lost his perspective. Nor did he hold a grudge against his brothers. After their father died, he told them, "You intended to harm me, but God intended it for good to accomplish what is now being done, the saving of many lives." He found the positive benefits in his negative experiences. And if he can do it, so can we.

WHAT ROLE DOES EXPERIENCE PLAY?

Experience plus honest self-examination leads to wisdom.

O ne of the most frustrating things for young leaders is having to wait to get their chance to shine. Leaders are naturally impatient, and I was no different. During the first ten years of my leadership, I heard a lot about the importance of experience. In my first position, people did not trust my judgment. They said I was too young and inexperienced. I was frustrated, but at the same time I understood their skepticism. I was only twenty-two years old.

After I led for a couple of years, people began to take notice of me. They saw that I had some ability. In my third year as a leader, a larger church considered me for their top leadership post. The position would have meant more prestige and better pay. But I soon found out that they had decided on an older, experienced leader. Once again, though disappointed, I understood.

At age twenty-five, I was nominated to become a member of my district's board. I was excited to be on the ballot. People my age were not usually considered for such a position. The election was close, but I lost to a well-respected veteran of our denomination.

"Don't worry," I was told. "Someday you will sit on that board. You just need a few more years of experience under your belt."

Time after time, my youth and inexperience were pointed out to me. And I was willing to pay my dues, learn my lessons, and wait my turn. As these more experienced people passed me, I would observe their lives to try to learn from them. I looked to see what kind of foundation they had built their lives on, which influential people they knew, how they conducted themselves. Sometimes I learned much by watching them. But many times I was disappointed. There were many people with years of experience under their belts but not much wisdom or skill to show for it.

That got me to wondering: *Why had experience helped some leaders and not others?* Slowly my confusion began to clear. What I had been taught all my life was not true: experience is not the best teacher! Some people learn and grow as a result of their experience; some people don't. Everybody has some kind of experience. It's what you do with that experience that matters.

HOW WILL EXPERIENCE MARK YOU?

We all begin our lives as empty notebooks. Every day we have an opportunity to record new experiences on our pages. With the turning of each page, we gain more knowledge and understanding. Ideally, as we progress our notebooks become filled with notations and observations. The problem is that not all people make the best use of their notebooks.

Some people seem to leave the notebook closed most of their lives. They rarely jot down anything at all. Others fill their pages, but they never take the time to reflect on them and gain greater wisdom and understanding. But a few not only make a record of what they experience; they linger over it and ponder its meaning. They reread what is written and reflect on it. Reflection turns experience into insight, so they not only live the experience but learn from it. They understand that time is on their side if they use their notebook as a learning tool, not just as a calendar. They have come to understand a secret. Experience teaches nothing, but evaluated experience teaches everything.

GAINING FROM EXPERIENCE

Do you know people who have lots of knowledge but little understanding? They may have means, but don't know the meaning of anything important? Even if they have a lot of know-how, they seem to possess little know-why? What is the problem with these individuals? Their life experience is void of reflection and evaluation. When twenty-five years go by, they don't gain twenty-five years of experience. They gain one year of experience twenty-five times!

If you want to gain from your experience—to become a wiser and more effective leader—there are some things about experience you need to know:

1. WE ALL EXPERIENCE MORE THAN WE UNDERSTAND

Baseball player Earl Wilson, the first black pitcher for the Boston Red Sox, quipped, "Experience enables you to recognize a mistake when you make it again." Let's face it: we're going to make mistakes. Too much happens to us in life for us to be able to understand all of it. Our experiences overwhelm our understanding. And no matter how smart we are, our understanding will never catch up with our experience.

So what is a person to do? Make the most of what we *can* understand. I do that in two ways. First, at the end of each day I try to remember to ask myself, "What did I learn today?" That prompts me to "review the page" of my notebook for the day. The second thing I do is take the last week of every year to spend time reviewing the previous twelve months. I reflect on my experiences—my successes and failures, my goals accomplished and dreams unmet, the relationships I built and the ones I lost. In this way, I try to help close some of the gap between what I experience and what I understand.

2. OUR ATTITUDE TOWARD UNPLANNED AND UNPLEASANT EXPERIENCES DETERMINES OUR GROWTH

Steve Penny, head of the S4 Leadership Network in Australia, observed, "Life is full of unforeseen detours. Circumstances happen which seem to completely cut across our plans. Learn to turn your detours into delights. Treat them as special excursions and learning tours. Don't fight them or you will never learn their purpose. Enjoy the moments and pretty soon you will be back on track again, probably wiser and stronger because of your little detour."

I must admit, having a positive attitude about life's detours is a constant battle for me. I prefer the expressway and a straight route to a winding scenic road. Anytime I find myself traveling on a detour, I'm looking for the quickest way out—not trying to enjoy the process. I know that's ironic for the guy who wrote *Failing Forward*, in which I wrote that the difference between average people and achieving people is their perception of and response to failure. Just because I know something is true and work to practice it doesn't mean it's easy.

In 2005, my close friend Rick Goad was diagnosed with pancreatic cancer. For one year I walked beside him through the uneven experiences created by this disease. In any given week, he would hope and be afraid, ask questions and find answers, have setbacks and possibilities. He endured a lot of ups and downs.

This experience was unexpected for Rick because he was still a young man—only in his forties. Throughout his ordeal I watched him live one day at a time, appreciate each moment, see the silver lining in the clouds, love his friends, and spend time with his God.

More than once he said to me, "John, I would not have chosen this for my life, but I also wouldn't trade this for anything."

Rick's detour ended in his death in 2006. It was heartbreaking. But Rick taught me and everyone else around him a lot during this difficult season. By watching him, we learned about how to live.

3. LACK OF EXPERIENCE IS COSTLY

At age sixty I now look back at my youth and I cringe at my naïveté. My toolbox of experience had only one tool in it: a hammer. If all you have is a hammer, everything looks like a nail. So I pounded and pounded. I fought many battles I shouldn't have. I enthusiastically led people down dead-end roads. I possessed the confidence that only the inexperienced can possess. I had no idea how little I knew.

Harry Golden remarked, "The arrogance of the young is a direct result of not having known enough consequences. The turkey that every day greedily approaches the farmer who tosses him grain is not wrong. It is just that no one ever told him about Thanksgiving."[1] I made plenty of mistakes as a young leader, but I was fortunate. None of them was disastrous. Most of the damage was self-inflicted, and the organizations I led didn't suffer terrible consequences for my inexperience.

4. Experience Is Also Costly

Lack of experience may be costly—but so is experience. It's a fact that you cannot gain experience without paying a price. The great American novelist Mark Twain once remarked, "I know a man who grabbed a cat by the tail and he learned 40 percent more about cats than the man who didn't." You just have to hope that the price is not greater than the value of the experience you gain, and sometimes you cannot judge what the price will be until after you have gained the experience.

Ted W. Engstrom, former president of World Vision, used to tell a story about the governing board of a bank who chose a bright, charming, young man to succeed their retiring bank president. The young man came to the old man to ask for help.

The conversation began, "Sir, what is the main thing I must possess to successfully follow you as president of this bank?"

The crusty old man replied, "The ability to make decisions, decisions, decisions."

"How can I learn to do that?" the young man asked.

"Experience, experience, experience," replied the retiring president.

"But how do I get experience?"

The old man looked at him and said, "Bad decisions, bad decisions, bad decisions."

It is as the old saying goes: experience gives the test first and the lesson later. The acquisition of experience can be costly. But it's not as costly as not gaining experience.

5. NOT EVALUATING AND LEARNING FROM EXPERIENCE IS MORE COSTLY

It's a terrible thing to pay the price for experience and not receive the lesson. But that is often what happens with people. Why? Because when an experience is negative, people often run away from it. They're very quick to say, "I'll never do that again!"

Mark Twain had something to say on this subject too. He observed, "If a cat sits on a hot stove, that cat won't sit on that hot stove again. In fact, that cat won't sit on a cold stove either." A cat doesn't have the mental capacity to evaluate his experience and gain from it. The best he can hope to do is follow his instinct for survival. If we want to gain wisdom and improve as leaders, we need to do better than that. We need to heed the words of *USA Today* founder Allen Neuharth, who said, "Don't just learn something from every experience. Learn something positive."

6. EVALUATED EXPERIENCE LIFTS A PERSON ABOVE THE CROWD

People who make it a regular practice to reflect on their experiences, evaluate what went wrong and right, and learn from them are rare. But when you meet one, you know it. There is a parable of a fox, a wolf, and a bear. One day they went hunting together, and after each of them caught a deer, they discussed how to divide the spoils.

The bear asked the wolf how he thought it should be done. The wolf said everyone should get one deer. Suddenly the bear ate the wolf.

Then the bear asked the fox how he proposed to divvy things up. The fox offered the bear his deer and then said the bear ought to take the wolf's deer as well.

"Where did you get such wisdom?" asked the bear.

"From the wolf," replied the fox.

The school of life offers many difficult courses. Some we sign up for willingly. Others we find ourselves taking unexpectedly. All can teach us valuable lessons, but only if we desire to learn and are willing to reflect on their lessons. If you are, what will be the result? You may exemplify the sentiment expressed by Rudyard Kipling in his poem "If":

If you can keep your head when all about you
Are losing theirs and blaming it on you,
If you can trust yourself when all men doubt you
But make allowance for their doubting too,
If you can wait and not be tired by waiting,
Or being lied about, don't deal in lies,
Or being hated, don't give way to hating,
And yet don't look too good, nor talk too wise:

If you can dream—and not make dreams your master,
If you can think—and not make thoughts your aim;
If you can meet with Triumph and Disaster
And treat those two impostors just the same;
If you can bear to hear the truth you've spoken
Twisted by knaves to make a trap for fools,
Or watch the things you gave your life to, broken,
And stoop and build 'em up with worn-out tools:

If you can make one heap of all your winnings
And risk it all on one turn of pitch-and-toss,
And lose, and start again at your beginnings
And never breathe a word about your loss;
If you can force your heart and nerve and sinew
To serve your turn long after they are gone,
And so hold on when there is nothing in you
Except the Will which says to them: "Hold on!"

If you can talk with crowds and keep your virtue,
Or walk with kings—nor lose the common touch,
If neither foes nor loving friends can hurt you;
If all men count with you, but none too much,
If you can fill the unforgiving minute
With sixty seconds' worth of distance run,
Yours is the Earth and everything that's in it,
And—which is more—you'll be a Man, my son!

Not only will you be a man—or woman—of integrity and wisdom, you will also benefit your people because you will be a better leader.

WHAT AM I WILLING TO GIVE UP
TO KEEP GROWING?

For everything you gain, you must give up something.

What is the key to going to the next level in your development? Put another way, what is the greatest obstacle you will face once you have begun achieving your goals and tasting success? I believe it is the ability to let go of what you have so that you can reach for something new. The greatest obstacle leaders face can be their own achievement. In other words, as Rick Warren says, "The greatest detriment to tomorrow's success is today's success."

In 1995, I faced one of the most difficult decisions of my life. I was twenty-six years into a highly successful career as a pastor. I was in as good a position as I could be. I was forty-eight years old and at the top of my game. The church I was leading, Skyline Wesleyan Church, was at that time the "flagship" church of the denomination. It had a national reputation and was highly influential. The church and I were highly respected. My reputation with the people was golden. I had spent more than a decade developing leaders, and the congregation was very solid. And it was in San Diego, California, one of the most beautiful cities in the country. It was ideal—both financially and professionally. I believe I could have settled in there and stayed until I retired. The only major obstacle that lay before me was the relocation of the church, which I believe we could have accomplished. (The leader who succeeded me has since accomplished it.)

I had only one problem. I wanted to go to the next level as a leader. I wanted to make a national and international impact. And I couldn't do it if I stayed there. I realized that the next stage of growth for me would require many difficult changes and much more time than I could give while leading the church. I understood that I needed to answer one critical question: am I willing to give up all that I have for a new level of growth?

What Is the Next Level Worth?

That's a question that every person must ask him- or herself more than once in a successful career. In *Leading Without*

Power, Max DePree wrote, "By avoiding risk, we really risk what is most important in life—reaching toward growth, our potential and a true contribution to a common goal."

I started learning this lesson about trade-offs as a child. My father would often admonish me by saying, "Pay now—play later." In fact, he said it a lot because I was someone who loved to play and *never* wanted to pay! What he was trying to teach me was to do the difficult things first, and then enjoy myself. I learned from him that we all pay in life. Anything we get will exact a price from us. The question is, when will we pay? The longer we wait to pay, the greater the price. It is like interest that compounds. A successful life is a series of trade-offs. In my career, over and over I have traded security for opportunity. I've given up what many would consider an ideal position so that I could grow as a leader or make a bigger impact.

I've found that the higher we go, the harder it is to make trade-offs. Why? We have so much more that we risk giving up. People often talk about the sacrifices they had to make in the beginning of their careers. But in truth, most people have very little to give up in the beginning. The only thing of value that they have is time. But as we climb higher, we have more, and we find it more difficult to let go of what we've worked for. That's why many climb partway up the mountain of their potential and then stop. They come to a place where they are unwilling to give up something in order to get the next thing. As a result, they stall—some forever.

As I debated the trade-offs of leaving the church to become a full-time writer, speaker, and developer of people, I sought advice from a few trusted mentors. One of them, author and consultant Fred Smith, passed on the following thoughts to me:

> Something in human nature tempts us to stay where we're comfortable. We try to find a plateau, a resting place, where we have comfortable stress and adequate finances. Where we have comfortable associations with people, without the intimidation of meeting new people and entering strange situations. Of course, all of us need to plateau for a time. We climb and then plateau for assimilation. But once we've assimilated what we've learned, we climb again. It's unfortunate when we've done our last climb. When we have made our last climb, we are old, whether forty or eighty.

That pushed me over the edge. I resigned. I would strive to go to a new level or fail trying!

What Will You Trade?

Soon after I resigned, I did some reflecting on the price of growth, and I wrote a lesson called "Ten Trade-Offs Worth Making." I believe the lessons I learned that have served me well may also serve you.

1. Trade Affirmation for Accomplishment

I've already explained that when I began my career, I was a people pleaser. I wanted approval from my followers, admiration from my peers, and awards from my superiors. I was an affirmation junkie. But accolades are like smoke that quickly fades away. Awards turn to rust. And financial rewards are quickly spent. I decided that I would prefer to actually get something *done* than to just make myself look good. That decision paved the way for most of the other trades I would make in life.

2. Trade Security for Significance

Success does not mean simply being busy. What you give your life to matters. The great leaders in history were great not because of what they owned or earned but because of what they gave their lives to accomplish. They made a difference!

I chose a career in which I expected to make a difference. But that did not exempt me from having to take risks to do things of greater significance. The same will be true for you, no matter what profession you have chosen.

3. Trade Financial Gain for Future Potential

One of life's ironies for me is that I was never motivated by money, yet Margaret and I ended up doing well financially. Why? Because I was always willing to put future potential ahead of financial gain.

The temptation is almost always to go for the cash. But this goes back to the idea of pay now, play later. If you are willing to sacrifice financially on the front end for the possibility of greater potential, you are almost always given greater chances for higher rewards—including financially.

4. Trade Immediate Pleasure for Personal Growth

If ever there was something our culture has a difficult time with, it is delayed gratification. If you look at the statistics on how much people are in debt and how little they put into savings, you can see that people are always seeking immediate pleasure.

When I was a kid, school bored me, and I couldn't wait to be done with it. I would have liked nothing better than to drop out, marry Margaret, my high school sweetheart, and play basketball. But because I wanted to have a career in leadership, I went to college, earned my degree, and waited until after graduation to marry Margaret. That was a *very long* four years.

Time after time, Margaret and I have put off or sacrificed pleasures, conveniences, or luxuries in order to pursue personal growth opportunities. We've never regretted it.

5. Trade Exploration for Focus

Some people like to dabble. The problem with dabbling is that you never really become great at anything. True, when you are young, you should try out new things—see where your strengths and interests lie. But the older you are, the more focused you should be. You can only go far if you specialize in something. If you study the lives of great men and women, you will find that they were very single-minded. Once you have found what you were created to do, stick with it.

6. Trade Quantity of Life for Quality of Life

I have to confess that I have a "more" mentality. If one is good, four is better. If somebody says he can hit a goal of twenty, I encourage him to reach for twenty-five. When I teach a one-hour leadership lesson on CD, I want to put so much content in it that the people who receive it will have to listen to it five times to get everything they can out of it.

Because of this natural inclination to do more, I've often had very little margin in my life. For years my calendar was booked solid, and I took very little time to relax. I remember asking my brother and his wife to come visit me, and Larry saying, "No, you're too busy. If we come, we won't ever see you."

I once read that the president of a large publishing company sought out a wise man to get his advice. After describing the chaos that was his life, he silently waited to hear something of value from the sage. The older man at first said nothing. He simply took a teapot and began pouring tea into a cup. And he kept pouring until the tea overflowed and began to cover the table.

"What are you doing?" the businessman exclaimed.

"Your life," responded the wise man, "is like a teacup, flowing over. There's no room for anything new. You need to pour out, not take more in."

It has been very difficult for me to change my mind-set from quantity to quality. Honestly, I'm still working on it.

Having a heart attack in 1998 certainly made an impact on me in this area. So did having grandchildren. I now carve out more time for the really important things in my life. I suggest you do the same.

7. Trade Acceptable for Excellent

This one is so obvious that it almost goes without saying. People do not pay for average. They are not impressed by anything that is merely acceptable. Leaders cannot rise up on the wings of mediocrity. If something is worth doing, give it your best—or don't do it at all.

8. Trade Addition for Multiplication

When people make the shift from doer to leader, they greatly increase the impact that their lives can make. It is a significant jump because, as I assert in *The 17 Indisputable Laws of Teamwork*, one is too small a number to achieve greatness. However, there is another jump that is more difficult and has even greater significance—changing from adder to multiplier.

Leaders who gather followers *add* to what they can accomplish. Leaders who develop leaders *multiply* their ability. How is that? For every leader they develop or attract, they gain not only that individual's horsepower but the horsepower of all the people that person leads. It has an incredible multiplying effect. Every great leader, regardless of where or when they led, was a leader of leaders. To go to the highest level of leadership, you must learn to be a multiplier.

9. Trade the First Half for the Second Half

In his book *Halftime*, Bob Buford says that most people who are successful in the first half of their life try to do the second half of their life in the same way. What he's really saying is that they reach a plateau and they are unwilling to trade what they have for a new way of doing things because it's much easier to stick with what's familiar.

If you are in the second half of life, you have probably spent much of your time paying the price for success. Don't waste it. Be willing to trade it for significance. Do things that will live on after you are gone. If you are in the first half, keep paying the price so that you have something to offer in your second half.

10. Trade Your Work for God for a Walk with God

As someone who has worked in ministry for many years, I understand the deep satisfaction of doing work that is for God. However, I also understand the trap of constantly doing *for* God without continually connecting *with* God.

If you are not a person of faith, then this may not make sense to you. However, if faith is a part of your life, remember that no matter how much value your work has, it cannot compare with a relationship with your Creator.

ARE YOU WILLING TO GIVE UP TO GO UP?

To achieve excellence, I think you have to learn to travel light. You must learn to off-load before trying to reload. You have to let go of one thing in order to grasp a new one. People naturally resist that. We want to stay in our comfort zone and hold on to what's familiar. Sometimes circumstances force us to give up something and we have the chance to gain something new. But more often than not, if we want to make positive trades, we have to maintain the right attitude and be willing to give up some things.

During the Civil War, President Abraham Lincoln was given a request for five hundred thousand additional recruits to fight in the army. Political advisors strongly recommended he turn it down since they thought honoring the request would prevent his reelection. But Lincoln's decision was firm.

"It is not necessary for me to be reelected," he said, "but it is necessary for the soldiers at the front to be reinforced by five hundred thousand men and I shall call for them. If I go down under the act, I will go down with my colors flying."

Lincoln is one of our greatest presidents because he was willing to give up everything—except final responsibility. That is the kind of attitude leaders need to have. Every new level of growth we hope to experience as leaders calls for a new level of change. You cannot have one without the other. If you want to be a better leader, get ready to make some trades.

As I've mentioned, I turned sixty in February of 2007. A few months before my birthday, I took the time to memorize the following prayer, because I wanted to pray it in the presence of my family and friends on my birthday. It says:

Lord, as I grow older, I think I want to be known as . . .
Thoughtful, rather than gifted,
Loving, versus quick or bright,
Gentle, over being powerful,
A listener, more than a great communicator,

Available, rather than a hard worker,
Sacrificial, instead of successful,
Reliable, not famous,
Content, more than driven,
Self-controlled, rather than exciting,
Generous, instead of rich, and
Compassionate, more than competent,
I want to be a foot-washer.

I'm still striving to become that person. I'm still making trades.

Now more than ever, I am aware that significant birthdays can either mark the passage of time, or they can mark changes we've made in our lives to reach our potential and become the person we were created to be. With each passing year, I want to make good choices that make me a better person, help me become a better leader, and make a positive impact on others. That requires a willingness to keep making trades, because for everything you gain, you have to give up something.

NOTES

CHAPTER 1

1. John C. Maxwell, *Breakthrough Parenting* (Colorado Springs: Focus on the Family, 1996), 116.
2. Denis E. Waitley and Robert B. Tucker, *Winning the Innovation Game* (Grand Rapids: Revell, 1986).

CHAPTER 2

1. Warren Bennis and Bert Nanus, *Leaders: The Strategies for Taking Charge* (New York: Harper Business, 2003), 56.
2. Longfellow, http://www.blupete.com/Literature/Poetry/Psalm.htm.
3. Jack Welch with Suzy Welch, *Winning* (New York: Harper Business, 2005), 61.

CHAPTER 4

1. Philip B. Crosby, *Quality Is Free: The Art of Making Quality Certain* (New York: Mentor Books, 1992), 68.

CHAPTER 5

1. Marcus Buckingham and Donald O. Clifton, *Now Discover Your Strengths* (New York: The Free Press, 2001), 6.

CHAPTER 6

1. David Bayles and Ted Orland, *Art and Fear: Observations on the Perils (and Rewards) of Artmaking* (Santa Barbara: Capra Press, 1993), 29.
2. Arthur Freeman and Rose Dewolf, *Woulda, Coulda, Shoulda: Overcoming Regrets, Mistakes, and Missed Opportunities* (New York: Harper Collins, 1992).
3. Patricia Sellers, "Now Bounce Back!" *Fortune*, 1 May 1995, 49.
4. Lloyd Ogilvie, *Falling into Greatness* (Nashville: Thomas Nelson, 1984).
5. Genesis 40:14–15 NIV.

CHAPTER 7

1. Harry Golden, *The Right Time: An Autobiography* (New York: Putnam, 1969).

ABOUT THE AUTHOR

JOHN C. MAXWELL is an internationally recognized leadership expert, speaker, and author who has sold over 16 million books. EQUIP, the organization he founded in 1996 has trained more than 2 million leaders worldwide. Every year he speaks to Fortune 500 companies, international government leaders, and audiences as diverse as the United States Military Academy at West Point, the National Football League, and ambassadors at the United Nations. A *New York Times, Wall Street Journal,* and *Business Week* best-selling author, Maxwell was named the World's Top Leadership Guru by Leadershipgurus.net. He was also one of only 25 authors and artists named to Amazon.com's 10th Anniversary Hall of Fame. Three of his books, *The 21 Irrefutable Laws of Leadership, Developing the Leader Within You,* and *The 21 Indispensable Qualities of a Leader* have each sold over a million copies.

Books by Dr. John C. Maxwell
Can Teach You How to Be A REAL Success

Relationships

Encouragement Changes Everything
25 Ways to Win With People
Winning With People
Relationships 101
The Treasure of a Friend
The Power of Partnership in the Church
Becoming a Person of Influence
Be A People Person
The Power of Influence
Ethics 101

Attitude

Self-Improvement 101
Success 101
The Difference Maker
How Successful People Think
The Journey From Success to Significance
Attitude 101
Failing Forward
Your Bridge to a Better Future
Living at the Next Level
The Winning Attitude
Be All You Can Be
The Power of Thinking Big
Think on These Things
The Power of Attitude
Thinking for a Change

Equipping

Teamwork 101
My Dream Map
Put Your Dream to the Test
Make Today Count
The Choice Is Yours
Mentoring 101
Talent is Never Enough
Equipping 101
Developing the Leaders Around You
The 17 Essential Qualities of a Team Player
Success One Day at a Time
The 17 Indisputable Laws of Teamwork
Your Road Map for Success
Today Matters
Partners in Prayer

Leadership

Leadership Promises For Your Work Week
Leadership Gold
Go for Gold
*The 21 Most Powerful Minutes
in a Leader's Day*
Revised & Updated 10th Anniversary
Edition of *The 21 Irrefutable
Laws of Leadership*
The 360 Degree Leader
Leadership Promises for Every Day
Leadership 101
The Right to Lead
The 21 Indispensable Qualities of a Leader
Developing the Leader Within You
The Power of Leadership

AVAILABLE NOW

New York Times Bestselling Author

JOHN C. MAXWELL

AUTHOR OF
THE 21 IRREFUTABLE LAWS OF LEADERSHIP

PUT YOUR
DREAM
TO THE TEST

10 QUESTIONS
to Help You See It *and* Seize It

Also available in audio and Spanish editions

Put Your Dream to the Test is a practical and inspiring
handbook that reveals the path for your future successes
of those who dared to live their dream.

MY
DREAM
MAP

An Interactive Companion to
Put Your Dream to the Test

Filled with practical applications and inspirational teaching, this companion book leads you through the process of clarifying your dream and finding the path to achieve it. *My Dream Map* also includes ample writing space for personal discovery.

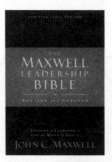

The Gold Standard for Leaders

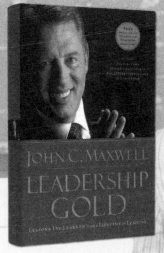